WE WEAR KICKS TO WORK

When Pop Culture Meets Leadership and Educations

Jeff Dess
Lenny A. Williams

Trill Or Not Trill Books

New York City, New York
Copyright 2020 Trill Or Not Trill Books

ISBN: 978-1-7357953-1-7

Printed in the United States of America

*Dedicated to the thousands of students
we've met around the world who continue to
inspire the world with with their brilliance,
aspiration all while rocking their favorite
kicks.*

Content

1.   Introduction

2.   We Wear Kicks To Work

3.   Middle Child Leadership

4.   Hidden Figures

5.   Appreciate Regular Degular Schmegular

6.   Learn How To Freestyle

7.   Pop Up University

8.   Clout Chasing Leadership

9.   Count Your Steps

10.   The Defiant Ones

11.   The Login Process

12.   The Marshawn Lynch Factor

13.   Don't Get Left

14.   The Students

15.   Pivot to Euro Step Leadership

TRILL
OR NOT
TRILL

INTRODUCTION

Let Urban Dictionary tell it and they'll define the term hater as *"a person that simply cannot be happy for another person's success, so rather than be happy they make a point of exposing a flaw in that person."*
That is a solid definition. It's one that Lenny and I grew up understanding. The meaning had some deep-rooted intention behind it. We try to avoid using the word "hater". For starters, allowing resentment and passionate dislike to have a home in your day to day life is unproductive. Secondly, hater has lost some of its luster. This isn't the same hip hop colloquialism found in so many of our favorite songs growing up. There was legitimate vitriol when used by anyone from rappers to the girl next door. When the Notorious B.I.G. sang about Playa Haters in 1997, he had them lay on the ground, turn their head round and he subsequently robbed them. The term has evolved into a lesser form of itself. Today, anyone can be a hater simply for disagreeing with an opinion or free thought. Haters have downgraded to people who don't like a Facebook post. At the time of this writing, the hashtag *#hatersgonnahate* has over 2.9 million posts. Most of them are carefully curated selfies.

If we rocked with the word hater as it was originally meant to be, then we would find out that higher education is filled with a bunch of them. The original definition may have transformed, but many of the sentiments and characteristics remain. Institutionally, professionally and personally, during our 20 plus years of service in the field, we have run into countless hater supervisors, hater leadership, hater faculty and more. Since we don't subscribe to that word though, something had to change. What we've been experiencing and saw happening to our students and colleagues required new terminology.

Detractors of Dopeness:
An individual who doesn't understand the appeal of others or their methods and in turn puts down and dismisses those alternative ideas.

These folks aren't haters but they are dangerous to your development. Ideas are a beautiful thing when cultivated. Detractors of Dopeness refuse to let you water those seeds of belief or intention. It is essential, in moments when plans are being put into motion, that you surround yourself with people who are willing to support your aspirational goals. The early days of an idea matter because this is the time when they either grow or wilt. Our students are faced with educators who shut them down from the start. We see students silenced on campuses all across the country because they look different, work with out of the box thinking and create colorful remixes to archaic truths. Our professional colleagues sit on plans and programs because their supervisors or institutions just don't see their dopeness.

While speaking at a conference in Denver, we met a Detractor of Dopeness. He was the CEO of one of the largest college speaking agencies in the country. We were just a one year old company. During dinner, our conversations included best practices, business plans and Kendrick Lamar versus JCole. He shared stories of his millionaire friends and told us that his biggest audiences were white male fraternity members. They were his key to success. When we brought up the integration of leadership and pop culture, he told us such a plan had no legs. When we let him know about a Kendrick Lamar vs JCole leadership program we were working on, he told us not enough "kids" knew who those people were. One of the biggest voices of leadership in the college market said any inclusion of pop culture in your work was not sustainable. Years later, we continue to bring the work to where the students reside.

Culturally Responsive Rejectors
These people do not care about displaying cultural competency while teaching or working. They never authentically

Culturally Responsive Teaching is a pedagogy that recognizes the importance of including students' cultural references in all aspects of learning outcomes. To keep the conversation going, we added a little twist to the theory to fit the world of higher education and leadership development. Trill EDU is a culturally responsive strategy to enhance the communication, leadership and career readiness skills of students, using their cultural references in all aspects of development.

We were called to work with an institution that was struggling with engagement. They particularly wanted to address their leadership speaker series. The institution is categorized as an urban school, located in a diverse industrial neighborhood. A majority of their students identify as Black and LatinX. After reviewing their list of previous presenters, we immediately saw some issues. From a list of 8 speakers, there were no speakers of color, there were no women and no speakers under the age of 50. When asked about the makeup of this group, the response was, "our experience and data lets us know what's best for the students. It's not the program that's the problem, but the attendance." We couldn't believe the type of response.

Our recommendations included more speakers of color, more women, student speakers and recent alumni. We were more intentional about the topics and even the titles. There was initial pushback because of our use of students and alumni. They were not big fans of pop culture references. We rolled out the plan, nonetheless. We used Instagram Live as a platform to reach different students and create additional viewing options. There was an immediate increase in unique attendees and returning participants. Time after time, we see educators who refuse to include the thought processes and experiences of their students within the curriculum or programming. Keeping out a culturally responsive strategy is a recipe for apathetic and disinterested students. Know that your students are learning the words to Pop Smoke songs and are binging shows like 13 Reasons Why.

We created Trill or Not Trill because calling out the different types of concerns is not enough. Reform and rejuvenation doesn't come from diagnosing the hater yourself. They must self-analyze to gain a surface level understanding of their contributions to archaic sensibilities. It requires those willing to make structural changes to systems that have been in place that sit comfortably as growth is stunted. Not embracing innovation will always serve as imprisonment of excellence. The following step is actual work.

WE WEAR KICKS TO WORK

I have been working in Higher Education for little over a decade and there are two things that continue to resonate. Despite the role or position students will always recognize authenticity. Additionally, the administration, no matter the level, will recognize deliverables. So, often the problem with our field is that in search for high level deliverables, we lose a grasp on the authentic sensibility as well as authentic connection to our students.

While preparing a presentation for the largest conference for Student Affairs and Higher Education professionals; National Association of Student Personnel Administrators (NASPA), we introduced the concept of Wearing Kicks to Work to hundreds of professionals in the field. Within the organization, their Innovative Programming Committee did a great job at opening the door for a broader conversation on the topic of continually seeking improvement through new and creative approaches. They define innovation through different viewpoints including *pedagogical, structural and technological that move practitioners toward more authentic and*

*relevant ways to teach, engage and support
students throughout their educational
trajectory.* Two key ideas that stand out to
me from this definition are **authentic** and
relevant ways to teach.

While assessing, we are often immersed in
statistics instead of the culture. To truly
innovate, one must find the connection to the
most innovative voices in the room and most
often, those people are our students. As we
continue to grow as professionals and get
promoted and gain higher positions of
leadership, oftentimes we start to disconnect
from the pulse of the campus and
consequently get removed from the spaces.
Best practices discussed in a boardroom and
found in peer reviewed articles are not
enough to innovate, particularly if most of
the voices in the room are disconnected. We
must remain relevant.

With that said, the moment I was promoted to
a place where committee meetings took up
more time than student engagement events, I
had to make sure my swag, as related to the
students and authentic relationships, wasn't
lost. Less time in the student union or
residence halls and more time in the rooms
with the big conference tables may mean

more structural work, but it doesn't always equate to innovation. My change was simple and proved to be incredibly valuable.

I started wearing Jordan's to work. I'm a low level sneakerhead[1] who never thought about rocking cool or exclusive kicks to the job, but it has moved the needle. Wearing dope sneakers is not only authentically part of who I am, but it is a strategic way to keep me locked into the pulse of the campus. We have several students from various backgrounds and micro communities who love sneakers. Beyond sneakers, there are those who celebrate their aesthetic accomplishments in multiple ways. Blue hair, fly eyebrows, fresh coats, exclusive henna tattoos and more, are all big-time features that help add to the innovation and authenticity of our university.

When I first threw on some Royal Blue Jordan 1's, the students were all in. Their energy within the educational space changed. On the other hand, there were colleagues who provided negative feedback. These are the people who are stunting innovation. While some professionals looked at my Jordan 1's as too bright, there were young black men

---

[1] An avid sneaker enthusiast

interacting with me who never spoke to me before. It was more than just sneakers; it was the connection after the kicks. It started with conversations about the latest sneaker drops which then morphed into educational experiences or student leadership positions. The president of our university complimented my Travis Scott 4's all while discussing student engagement and the implementation of leadership models. Sadly it was at that point that some colleagues started to get on board. To innovate is to disrupt the norm but to innovate as an educator is to not only disrupt, but teach and elevate the students while doing so.

Wearing dope sneakers has helped me link up with students who weren't open to leadership opportunities. We talk about coolest hypebeast[2] Instagram accounts and follow that up with student programming strategies. As I leave events and head into more of those meetings, students are still dapping me up and asking about the latest shoe drops. We talk about their shoes, whether new or old, which opens the door into unofficial retention

---

[2] slang word for someone, usually a man, who follows trends in fashion, particularly streetwear, for the purpose of making a social statement.

practices. NASPA, as an organization, has set the conference dress code as business casual. This is more than suggested attire. It is an opportunity to intersect aspects of professionalism, authenticity and swag. We as educators should take this from the conference to the student union and right up to the administrative buildings.

Consumption and Consumerism

This is a dialogue that goes beyond the sneakers on your feet. As educators, where are you finding the alternative connections to your students? Traditional icebreakers break the ice but don't create impactful long standing relationships. You can ask someone how they're doing or where are they from, but if it isn't authentic you'll lose out on connecting to any student. The interactions that last are those with the intention to create a longstanding developmental growth.

As professionals, is there a state of relatedness with those you supervise or work with? For some, it is a hairstyle or cool lapel pin on a blazer. I've seen people who rap and others who wear colorful outfits to a black and white campus. Don't add flavor for your own selfish ways of standing out. That lack of authenticity will easily get flushed out and subsequently called out. Connecting to the pulse requires intentionality from those in leadership. Institutions, companies and organizations are continually taking archaic steps in a world where students and innovative professionals are flying around. Aesthetics matters. Swag matters. Innovation matters. What are you doing to change the narrative of connecting to those you are leading? Moving the conversation to new heights requires a structural change in language.

Consumption and consumerism are two terms that come to mind when discussing the sneaker game. Often in the field of education, we find leaders shying away from those ideas. There is fear to include business terminology in educational spaces. They are not the boogeymen. In fact, embracing such entities is essential to the growth and development of our students. Before my time in higher education, my background was working at a corporation within sales and marketing. The first statement shared to the team was "the customer is always right." One lesson from a sales training a few years ago, spoke to understanding what drives the consumer. In the exercise, we had to observe pictures and items within a consumer's workspace that might lead to this individual buying specific products. In education, this activity is transferrable as it provides a look on how higher education can pay closer attention to the programming needs, retention efforts and engagement approaches for all students. Numbers are essential but the feelings of the constituents are equally as important to success. Are we understanding them beyond assessments and meetings? Are we adding relevant cultural references as examples in the educational process? When a student wears their Chipotle uniform to class every day, did it ever come across to you that their lack of attendance to events is because of a demanding work schedule? Answering these questions requires a type of vision that speaks to and translates inside and outside the classroom. The fact that the customer is always right doesn't mean that the student is always right, but it does mean creating a student-centered environment is mandatory.

As we take on roles as leaders, we must empower our students' interests and strengths to keep them coming back. It goes back to the sneaker game. As consumption increases, the maker of the sneakers includes additional cultural references and changes to keep the sneakers, whether new or revisited, relevant to what's happening now. Kyrie Irving released a new brand of shoes inspired by, and including designs from, SpongeBob Squarepants. NBA MVP, Giannis Antetokuounmpo, has signature sneakers referencing the classic film, *Coming to America.* Even Nike and Jordan's took a culturally responsive step by partnering with platinum selling rapper, Travis Scott. Their collaboration has produced one of the hottest sneakers in the game. Our students are customers, paying for opportunities and enhancement. They are looking for the best and potentially life changing experiences possible. It is our responsibility as educators to elevate the product.

The Practice of Wearing Kicks to Work

Wearing kicks to work is a theory we use to represent the idea of challenging norms in a culturally responsive way. It is meant to serve as a model for the implementation of structural change within any archaic space. Not every institution, workplace or area of development will be open to change. We need leaders who are willing to take progressively incremental steps towards an eventual large-scale shift.

There are some early steps one can take when looking to wear their own Kicks to Work.

1. Divorce traditional styles
When we get engaged to archaic systems, we end up marrying mediocrity. The divorce process is simple. Be honest about how outdated your spaces are and begin the process of walking away. There is no need to rip off the band aid. Identify each target area and slowly make the structural shifts. When it comes to dress codes, allow people to rock those Jordan's or create a comfortable day for kicks. I've worked with teams that implemented casual dress days which then transformed into casual dress weeks. Reexamine hours of operation to maximize

unique situations that exist in your space. Furniture and physical space layouts and hierarchical structure are all aspects that can go stale. They are also areas to begin the divorce process. Start the conversations with your Human Resources department and implement.

2. Be open to dialogue

Your job description should never include "being the only voice in the room." Knowledge isn't a private dinner and is best served buffet style. As a leader it's your job to create opportunities for people to feel comfortable with having new conversations. Sentiments of anxiety or nervousness will always exist unless you make room for dialogue. I've recently turned some of our traditional staff meetings into bagged lunch innovation sessions. Our only agenda item is about innovating your areas or the team.

3. Lead by example

As a leader you are considered a role model and a representation of your team. Leadership, however, is not a solo act as a team must all carry the load together. Leaders who stand in the spotlight during tough times earn the hearts of their teammates. But even more respect is earned by being your authentic self. For us, wearing sneakers and adding culture into our work is our authenticity. We are not asking you to wear sneakers literally, but on figurative level that is a clear representation of your authenticity in leadership.

Favorite Jordan's

We would be remiss if we didn't share a list of favorite Jordan's.

Off white Jordan 1

Success can be repeated and disrupted. If you know us by now, we suggest disruption when talking innovation. Here, we have the most popular Jordan for over 20 years getting a makeover. It's time to look at our success make sure we are innovating.

Jordan 10s

This unique shoe listed Jordan's accomplishment on the sole of the shoe. As a leader, build a winning environment. Whether it's actual items in your office or actual people that enjoy success. Success breeds success. It's also ok to be reminded of the work you have accomplished for the days you get down. Protect your energy.

Jordan 1 (Banned)

As a leader, a new idea may come with caution. Sometimes, colleagues may be hesitant about new ideas or, even worse, say things such as, "That won't work" "We tried that before" "I don't think it's allowed. The story goes that Michael Jordan was fined $5,000 by the NBA every time he wore the shoes during their debut in 1984 because they broke the league's uniform rules. Nike capitalized on this, creating an ad campaign that played on that forbidden fruit quality. Sometimes, as a leader, when innovating we need to sit on the edge of breaking a rule but the success lies on the other end. Jordan

Jordan Travis Cactus Jack 4s

Blending of two worlds; entertainment and athletics, created an unforgivable sneaker. As an educator, it reminds me to continue finding nontraditional partnerships when being innovative within a space. We avoid remaining stagnant by continuing to build with new voices outside of our realm of comfort and regularity

MIDDLE CHILD LEADERSHIP

To be in touch with the community requires
one to coexist with as many of its members
as possible. We can't lead if we're too busy
criticizing new voices or ideas because they
don't match the frequency and flavor of the
old. These old school, get off my porch
attitudes have no place in leadership. To
reach new heights requires a full
understanding of diversity. One must be
prepared to grasp the range of individuality
and generational differences. Doing so means
increasing your awareness level of how
varied your audiences will be. This is what
we call Middle Child Leadership. It is an
ability to lead across generations while
possessing a commitment to communicating
to everyone in the room.

JCole's hit song, *Middle Child* released in
2019, encompasses the idea of leading
intergenerationally. Hip Hop star, JCole, has
recorded songs with classic hip hop artists
like Missy Elliott, Jay-Z, Kanye West and
The Game. He's rocked out with generational
peers like Drake, Kendrick Lamar and Wale.
We've also seen him drop some bars on
tracks with Cozz, J.I.D. and 21 Savage, who

are all younger than he is. This is the versatility we need in our leadership spaces.

When multiple generational voices are in the room, we have the ability to time travel. Middle Child Leadership allows you the opportunity to educate about the past, exist in the present and elevate into the future. Learn the languages of different eras and you'll be able to speak to the world from a perspective. JCole's verses provide more lessons on how to exist and communicate to all types audiences. Here are a few examples of how Cole's bars can serve as leadership tools.

I'm dead in the middle of two generations I'm little bro and big bro all at once

Middle Children see it all. They can absorb the lessons from older siblings while providing guidance to the younger ones. The Middle Child is a liaison between two generations. To enhance your ability of reaching multiple voices, you require attention paid to the elevation of your communication skills. Being able to articulate expectations or share your goals effectively, regardless of the generation or other characterizations, will allow a more manageable navigation through your audience. We want to eliminate as much confusion as possible when attempting to create cross generational communicative goals. This line is about the awareness of his place within the rap game. The more deeply connected you are to your identity, the more you'll be able to understand where you stand among others within your space. Defining your role will help you become more accurate in delegating tasks and identifying responsibilities.

"This watch came from Drizzy, he gave me a gift
Back when the rap game was prayin' I'd diss
They act like two legends cannot coexist"

Throughout Middle Child, he addresses conflict management. This line shows how peers who exist in the same generation can seem to have problems because of rumors. Cole states that people wanted him to diss Drake. As a leader, moments will arise where you're given an opportunity to take a shot at a rival or say something disparaging about a staff member or colleague who doesn't agree with your ways. Don't fall for this trap. Stay the course towards success. Work on developing a specific leadership plan with a vision, goals and outcomes. Unbiased structure places an onus on the content and the group as whole. This will help you focus on how your content and work will enhance others. I experienced some unsaid behind the door criticism with my staff. My experience and age were being challenged on a regular basis and this was spreading throughout the office. My initial reaction was to confront this person head on. Instead, I created a strategic game plan for the office. Everyone's needs were considered. Timelines and progress steps were on full display and I held open door hours with the staff to discuss their objections. Room was made to clear the air, but the strategic plan had to be a part of the conversation. In your spaces of leadership, perceived notions can't be the most present voice in the room. Imaginary beef will grow into actual problems the more it festers. A recent article about the *15 ways Millennials do this* or *the 12 reasons Gen Z don't do this*, can go from the page to the office. Be the person that squashes the potential cross generational problem. Create intentional opportunities for face to face opportunities to enhance team communication. Bring people to the table and create collaborative projects.

A true Middle Child Leader will worry less about how others perceive them generationally, but more so use their generational background as a conduit for success.

"Everything grows/It's destined to change/ I love you lil' ni**as/ I'm glad that you came"

I love working with new staff members. Younger views entering the arena add necessary excitement. When JCole says everything grows and is destined to change, that includes your office. The people who are bringing this type of energy are either new members or younger ones. Embrace a tone that might not be mirror images of your experiences. When saying *I'm glad that you came*, Cole is speaking to the new rappers. He shows them love in a world expecting them to beef over difference of styles. By shouting them out in the fashion, it's not just acknowledgment, but also respect for the changes being brought to the table. Don't settle and keep younger voices out of the conversation of development. Less experience doesn't equate to less innovation or inefficient outlook. Expand the conversation and be openly thankful for any input brought upon by people, no matter the generation.

In creating a recent strategic plan for my office, I looked for advice from older mentors and sat down with the youngest members of my staff, as well as our students. Everyone's input was considered when creating goals, outcomes and initiatives. One can't expect to change without multigenerational inclusion. When writing new reports, I've included staff members as contributors, even if what they added was not the largest part of the document. It shows them that, "I'm glad that you came." These are also great moments of professional development

"To the OG's /I'm thanking you now/ Was watching you when you was paving the ground / I copied your cadence / I mirrored your style / I studied the greats/ I'm the greatest right now"

We see here, another case of JCole's acknowledgement of a generation. OG stands for original gangster, but ultimately is a term of endearment for those who are veterans or provide old school insight. He thanks those who came before him and talks about how his own style couldn't have been created without their influence. It's easy to think as a leader your changemaking ideas and forward moving plans had nothing to with those before you. Have meaningful conversations with your team and staff who have more years at the workplace. This helps in avoiding making the same mistakes over and over. Their insight gives you a glimpse into what worked well or what needs to be changed or removed.

"Just left the lab with young 21 Savage"

Be intentional about your processes being cross generational in the planning. Work and directly collaborate with generations younger than yours. Identify the spaces of intersectionality and embrace the differences while celebrating the similarities. When taking on a role of leadership, you immediately become a mentor. Take your mentorship to the next level by becoming a collaborator.

"I'm 'bout to go and meet Jigga for lunch"

Don't ever underestimate the importance of wisdom. Learn how to navigate hurdles by listening to the stories of how people tripped on their journey. Schedule regular meetings over dinner or tea with a member from a generation older than you. Provide insight while soaking up valuable information. At my institution there are particular staff members and faculty who I meet with consistently. Even when lunch meetings are tough, we agree to both attend the next event or university wide meeting and sit next to each other.

Had a long talk with the young nigga Kodak / Reminded me of young niggas from 'Ville / Straight out the projects, no fakin', just honest / I wish that he had more guidance, for real

Middle Child Leaders can't just sit idly by. It's easy to criticize, but the real work is to mentor and assist in the healing process. The Middle Child Leader can get through to difficult exteriors and bridge gaps, free of judgement.

Making people feel welcome will never be enough, the real work comes with authentic collaborative behavior. Such intergenerational collaboration requires intentional strategies by the leaders in the room. One of the most effective methods of doing so is to create co-leadership opportunities.

4 Questions to Help You Become a Better Middle Child Leader

- Are you willing to create a space that is open to work/life balance, while also celebrating those who put in extra hours?

- Are you willing to change the culture of the office or space by including multiple viewpoints?

- Are you prepared to make important phone calls AND communicate via text message?

- Have you created spaces where multiple generations are in the room having face to face to interactions as a group?

3 of Our Favorite JCole Songs Made to Inspire Leadership

Let Nas Down

"And it's hard for the great to tell somebody how to be great"

The first word that comes to mind is *vulnerability*. As a leader, it is imperative to admit and share times of weakness, even in a public setting. It is a way for leaders to earn trust from those they lead. In this song, JCole showed his human side by letting a mentor know that although he let him down, the work was still being done. As leaders, we must show our human side but also allow our mentees to make mistakes. Every mistake is one step outside of your comfort zone, closer towards success.

Crooked Smile

"And if you need a friend to pick you up, I'll be around and we can ride with the windows down, the music loud I can tell you I aint laughed in a while But I wanna see that crooked smile"

This song is a tale of how you can overcome your insecurities. We must embrace our own insecurities before looking to help anyone else. Leaders should also create safe spaces and resources for those going through these dark times. We must always provide light in the room.

Love Yourz

"Always gon' be a whip that's better than the one you got/Always gon' be some clothes/That's fresher than the ones you rock."

For most of our readers, especially those within education, we must provide love and support to our space on a daily basis. Unfortunately for many of us, that comes with a sacrifice of long hours, carrying others energy and low pay. We must be reminded of the reason we work here and what ultimately brings us happiness. In this very touching song, JCole reminds us all that happiness is deeper than material objects, status, and perception. As leaders, we can't help anyone without loving ourselves and remaining within our passions throughout the day to day.

HIDDEN FIGURES

Hidden Figure Leaders are powerful individuals on campuses and spaces that we typically forget because of their lack of exposure, unceremonious titles and more. As educators in a world filled with budget cuts and high turnover rates, we must utilize every resource around us. As we lose talented staff to other opportunities, remember to look everywhere for your change agents. You have legitimate leaders right in front of you. They are nontraditional in a sense, but they are among the most knowledgeable in the space. The administrative assistant or secretary often knows the ins and outs of the office and the issues of the people who walk through its doors better than anyone else. The housekeeping staff have served as counselors. The security guard has been a life coach and the dining hall chef has done unofficial assessment on the needs of the community. Actions will always speak louder than titles. Hidden Figure Leaders understand the unseen pulse that often dictates all that is around them.

Hidden Figure Leader: John Smith

"You already know," is a saying that resonates throughout the campus of New Jersey City University. This phrase is part of the daily routine for a man named John Smith. John is someone that exhibits leadership through humor, empathy and authenticity with an infectious personality. To many senior leaders, John is just another EOF (state-funded program for low-income college students) counselor, but to students and fellow employees, he holds a position greater than the school's president. True Hidden Figure leaders are never limited by their title or position. He continually goes beyond his job description because of his passion and students first mentality. While many counselors often stay behind the four walls or a desk, John is the opposite; you can catch him in every space occupied by students. As a result, his job becomes mobile. Students are always willing to meet with him because he is always willing to meet them where they are at. He is comfortable in any space.

Not only is John a Hidden Figure Leader, but he also empowers others to recognize and become hidden figure leaders as well. He will link students with other non-traditional leaders on campus such as housekeepers, security officers and food service staff members, by connecting personality traits and backgrounds (neighborhood, religion, culture, sports interests, etc.) to achieve accountability on both sides. For example, as a first-generation student, John linked me to a security guard named Garfield. At the time, as a mentor, John was explaining to me the importance of being well read. I mentioned not finding books that piqued my interest and in turn he connected me to the security guard who read every single day. You both come from a similar background and interest so let's make the introduction. After a few conversations, Garfield turned into a mentor who provided specific book recommendations in business and history. The relationship helped improve my grades and morale. In turn, Garfield took this mentorship and turned it into self-motivation and inspiration. He would proceed to start his own college career one semester after we met.

"You already know" is a staple to live by for all of us. Many of us know the culture, setting, students, or employees in our space, but we limit ourselves due to titles or positions. It is time to get up from the confinement of four walls, by using every resource possible to become the most authentic culturally responsive leader there is. For the traditional leaders, I challenge you to identify and empower the hidden figures in your space.

Hidden Figure Leader: Mr. Amoo

While working at an institution in Brooklyn, my first month living in a residence hall with close to 1000 college students was met with drama, loudness, excitement, education and more. There was consistent voice throughout. He knew about everything. Every student's name, their concerns, their habits and characteristics was second nature. His name was Mr. Amoo or as the students called him, just Amoo. He served as the security guard. His calming voice would be heard over the noise. His favorite phrase was "do the right thing." It was a mantra that every student living in that building knew about. They cried to him and he listened as people struggled financially. He joked with students about their roommates. He counseled them when their relationships were a bit choppy. As an immigrant, he related to the students with accents or their parents from other countries. He observed, taught and led, all while sitting at his post. The man was a culturally responsive leader who, in the eyes of administration, was just a competent security officer. Amoo went beyond the requirements of his duties and was committed to the stories of other people's family, culture, personality and, overall, their stories. In return, the audience experience is elevated. Safe spaces are created in alternative locations.

I left the school and wouldn't see Amoo for years. One day I stopped by the campus and he said "I hope you're doing the right thing." He remained consistently dedicated to the feelings and aspirations of others.

It was shared with me that he passed away soon after our final brief encounter. One of my former students posted,

"Sad to hear at LIU, we lost another great motivational person. A person who at some day, gave key advice, a joke or simply just told us to do the right thing. A person who speaks every day, whether we're upset, sad and or happy. He had seen us come in as

freshmen and leave as graduates. Rest in Peace Amoo."

Soon the thread grew to hundreds of students sharing their experience with Amoo or the advice he had given them. Such an outpour is a display of how impactful culturally responsive relationships can be. By typical standards, he did his job as a leader, he changed lives.

How to Elevate Hidden Figures

While watching the film Hidden Figures, I kept wondering how this wasn't a larger part of the fabric of our history. These brilliant black women scientists not only had their work hidden during their time as professionals, but their stories were kept mostly in the dark, until a book published in 2016. It is unacceptable to have such major figures hidden for this long.

Our fellow educator and brother, Chris Emdin once stated, *"Every young person has a story to tell. Schools obscure those stories. Society buried them even deeper. The best teachers unearth them."* This sentiment goes beyond the classroom. It's arrogant to believe success can happen with voices being drowned. We can't be culturally responsive by ignoring and leaving important narratives behind. It requires true efforts from people willing to sacrifice and lead. Our team at Trill or Not Trill uses a few methods to assure Hidden Figure Leaders are not only being heard, but are part of the conversation.

Appreciate
Sometimes the Hidden Figure might not only feel unseen but can often feel undervalued.

Build morale within the entire space, and particularly with that individual, by showing appreciation for the acts that often go unnoticed. The small wins count too. This person may not be in the forefront, but their work is part of the success within the office. We talk about openly celebrating a bit later, but in this case, it's just about recognizing the work they do. It's about knowing people's names and never devaluing the person because of who they are, where they are from or what they do.

Be open to Unconventional.
Hidden Figures usually have nontraditional approaches to connecting. Be open to styles that may not be conventional but are effective. Let their mode of connection flourish. We've seen bonds created with students over a sports team eventually turn into a conversation about leadership. One of our IT staff members was known to set up the technology for all the events. He was also an avid e-Sports player. During his off time or while walking through the halls, he'd bond with students by giving tips on certain games. He reached an audience of students who were not always being paid attention to.

Openly celebrate
Recognize and celebrate the accomplishments of the Hidden Figures. Do so publicly and use this as an example of how we can impact in different ways. At the annual student awards ceremony for an institution I worked in, we gave away an unsung hero award. In my time, that honor has been given to janitors, professors, bookstore cashiers, administrative assistants and cafeteria chefs.

APPRECIATE REGULAR DEGULAR SCHMEGULAR

I am a big fan of Cardi B. As college educators with about 25 years of combined experience, we've met Cardi Bs over and over again in the residence halls or expressing herself at a club meeting. Belcalis Almanzar (Cardi B's real name) has been in our Creative Writing or Entrepreneurship courses before. The Bodak Yellow star has never personally crossed paths with either of us, but so many students over the years fit the model. As she's described herself, I've known plenty of self-proclaimed "regular degular schmegular girls from the Bronx," Brooklyn, Jersey City, Philly and beyond.

We've worked at predominantly White Institutions, urban institutions as well as public and private schools. At each of these stops, there were Cardi Bs around. Most of them were first-generation college students or from areas where college wasn't always the first option for success. They felt way more comfortable speaking slang than the Ol' Queen's English. They were mostly young black and brown women who may have struggled initially in classes, but were sharp in so many other ways. Their personalities were large and infectious to the student body despite not holding traditional leadership positions.

These young ladies were also heavily judged by staff, faculty and peers who weren't willing to do the work and meet the students where they were. Whether coming from great backgrounds or abusive relationships, stereotyping happens because there are educators who aren't willing to create a welcoming and affirming environment. These students are historically marginalized and it is our duty to leave the judgment at the door.

I've heard all the following from colleagues and other educators in describing students who they perceived to be a certain way.

- We can't hire her as an orientation leader because of how many times she said the word "Yo" during a group interview.
- I don't know if this is true, but I heard she's sleeping with half of the basketball team.
- She seems smart but she's kind of ghetto.

- She's a bit too loud and aggressive for me.

This is destructive behavior that happens all the time. Cardi B has heard some of this same critique; not on a campus but because of her interviews, Instagram posts or Love and Hip Hop appearances. The negative connotation associated with strippers and exotic dancers also brought on criticism towards her character.

Cardi flipped it though.

It turned into New York Times articles, performing at the MTV Video Music Awards, all while being praised by Demi Lovato and meeting the likes of Beyoncé. She was the first female rapper to reach the top of Billboard charts without any other billed acts since Lauryn Hill in 1998. She continues to sign major endorsements and is one of the biggest stars in the world.

 She started to pop and outlet after outlet fell in love or wanted a ticket to the Cardi B bandwagon.

Through hard work and taking advantage of opportunities presented to her, she's parlayed viral Instagram fame into international recognition and success. Once regarded as "just a stripper from the Bronx," today she's the hottest commodity in pop culture. Many of those students don't get the Cardi B treatment despite efforts to be their best selves and shut down unfair perceptions. Unintentional, or sometimes intentional, sexist, racist and classist mentalities from educators keep them from gaining opportunities.

I've witnessed educators, and so many others, criticize every single aspect of Cardi B's life. Sucka MC Educators, as we call them, have trouble recognizing raw authenticity. There will always be people described as a bit rough around the edges. Sucka MC Educators get mad at folks who've only had steak from Applebee's and have never had filet mignon. Instead of introducing new opportunities and experiences, they judge and condemn. The pressure is on to examine and bring out strengths and get deeper with the learning process. Cardi B could run and win a city council position. She was one of my favorite

Resident Assistants and student leaders on campus. Cardi B could be sitting on university committees. Bodak Yellow could be Bodak Ph.D. or Bodak MBA or simply Bodak Yellow. All of which are wins.

Sucka MC Educators seem to forget their own flaws as they throw stones from their poorly constructed glass houses. Cardi B isn't perfect but who cares? It'll be those same Sucka MC Educators who were singing about having bloody shoes or watching Cardi on the big screen that will not appreciate the regular shmegular. Cut it out.

I pay my mama bills, I ain't got no time to chill - Cardi B

LEARN HOW TO FREESTYLE

Trill or Not Trill has always incorporated Hip Hop into the leadership and educational work. I mean, we named our institute after a word popularized by UGK. We see how this cultural phenomenon is bigger than some beats and bars. Kendrick Lamar's music has been featured on our presentation slides. Swag surfin' is a daily routine at most of our talks. Hip Hop elevates the voice of the voiceless and is constantly making something out of nothing. There are five key elements that historically defined the essence of hip hop. DJing, rapping, break dancing, graffiti art and knowledge are the historical core tenets that helped birth the culture. In the world of public speaking, it's essential to have some of the similar qualities of an emcee/rapper. One has to be a storyteller and use wordplay creatively when necessary. You may have prepared written statements but always be ready to improvise.

Within rap, freestyling is a quality that has helped define some of the best emcees, whether they were on the radio, the block or in the cafeteria.

Freestyle is an improvisational form of rapping with or without beats in the background. Whether people are particularly skilled or not, the essence of "coming off the dome" or making it up as you go, is an energetic experience. In its nature, freestyling pushes the norm to the creative edge.

Freestyle Leadership is the ability to adapt to as many student experiences as possible. Such a frame of thought explores differences and encourages the educator to not only be open to unexpected changes, but embrace them. It assures a nature of spontaneity that won't trap you inside a traditional bubble or framework. "*Many educators still believe that good teaching transcends place, people, time, and context.*" *(Geneva Gay)*. Believing that you can lead and educate in the same way to the various types of audiences is an ineffective approach. Such behavior carelessly glosses over the uniqueness attributed to audiences from different areas. What freestyling does is it allows for diversity to exist during any type of process. Sometimes the plan has to change on the fly. It's imperative that you are prepared. We once walked into a college campus ready to speak about traditional leadership to a group of seniors. The slides were ready to go but the audience had a different feeling. Conversations on the side before the talk alerted me that the young folks were very much concerned about life after graduation and getting jobs. Going the route, which was expected, would certainly lead to disappointment, so we came to an agreement to flip the script. The speech was now about leadership with a focus on career development and life planning.

A freestyle leader is one who puts the people first and cares about bonds being formed in as many ways as possible. They work towards making sure the plan of action is connected to as many people as possible. Discussions become more organic because everything and everyone around you is involved. *To effectively do so requires you to have more than one playbook in your backpack.* Study different styles to avoid being stagnant and stale in your work. Having a singular style of leadership lacks ingenuity and stunts progress. *You must also know your audience and pay attention to your surroundings.* Successfully freestyling "off the top of the dome" will always include reaching into the crowd for resources and extra thoughts. In a society where the environments are ever changing, we need tools to help us interpret, adapt and respond.

We brought the art of freestyle to some of our talks in an activity we call The Closers. At the end of the keynote speech, we invited five students to the stage. Having no idea what they were getting into, some were nervous and others were excited. The audience at large buzzed watching their peers become a part of the experience. We proceeded to ask the participating individuals to give us a word that relates to the talk they just heard. You never know what you're going to get. People have given us everything from discipline, excellence and motivation, to apples, drugs and Rihanna. Our jobs would be to freestyle a micro speech, one minute in length, based off the term. It never goes perfect, but it always energizes the crowd. We make call backs to ideas from the earlier speech, incorporate song lyrics, include the audience all within the one minute. The spontaneity, although nerve wracking, always produced new content. Students walked away being a part of the speech themselves.

Freestyling has a second definition that was birthed prior to the meaning of improvised rapping. It also means writing but not sticking to one topic. The popular 80's era rapper, Kool Moe Dee, defines freestyling in his book, *There's a God on the Mic* as, "From a leadership perspective, this is a display of mastery over multiple areas. It demonstrates that we have done our homework in multiple areas and not just a string of random disjointed ideas. The real display of talent is the ability to reach as many audiences as you anticipated would be listening. We often know going into situations who our audience will be, but outliers and unexpected participants and listeners always show up. You never know how anyone will respond to your work, but these new faces create a whole new challenge.

One recent example of the other type of freestyle comes from the super dope MC known as Black Thought. To some, he's known as the front man for the band on Late Night with Jimmy Fallon. To others he's one of coldest most skillful rappers to ever grab a mic. Long time DJ and radio host, Funkmaster Flex, is known to invite rappers to his show and freestyle in the way that Kool Moe Dee defines. Black Thought came to the studio and tore it down. Although not off the top, his bars created similar feelings of spontaneous combustion. He was fully prepared with his rhymes, as we need to be with our lessons and theories. Some of our favorite lines of his serve as perfect devices to assist in becoming more culturally responsive.

OGs and young lions equally proud to listen. The secret amalgamism of algorithm
As we mentioned when discussing Middle Child Leadership, it's imperative to be able to reach multiple generations. Make everyone proud by including multiple voices. Figuring out the algorithm takes strategy, but also gets a variety of voices in the room. Let's lead for them all.

Them brothers said, "Don't go from written bars filled with rage. / To primetime television and your gilded cage/ Then forget it's people in the world still enslaved."
No matter how far your career elevates or the amount of degrees acquired, remember where you came from. We were all students at one point and we needed help. The learning process is always in effect even as you grow professionally. Don't leave anyone behind because of your status or ego.

POP UP UNIVERSITY

When my cousin Bart, a former basketball legend in his neighborhood, asked me to hoop, I knew it was time to bring the A game. On arrival everyone dapped us and gave handshakes. Bart was the main man, which immediately gave me entry into a group that doesn't always trust newcomers. As the game went along, my skills opened more doors towards camaraderie. The biggest door opened though, when Bart told me that the quick guard on my team wanted to go to college and wanted to become an entrepreneur but was struggling with his choices. I was introduced to Manny who was only 15 years old. "Yo Manny, my cousin works at a college." That introduction was all I needed to turn a basketball court into a pop-up University. The conversation led to tips on college, alternatives to college and entrepreneurship. I became not only the professor, but the student as well. I took tips on why Manny did not like his traditional school setting. He told me what was missing for students like him who wanted success but was failing within the typical school space.

Pop Up Universities find value in every space. Education can't stop because there aren't any chalkboards, desks or chairs. There is no one size fits all methodology of teaching. As educators, we can become superheroes in all spaces. Understanding the value of our knowledge and resources can change an entire person or community.

Fast forward, Manny is now an entrepreneur in that same area, running an annual basketball tournament on the same court. He credits our talk, or better yet our *Pop Up U* in helping him gain confidence, assess options and research ideas to help reach his personal success.

Pop Up U is the ultimate opportunity to meet individuals and potential students in spaces they are comfortable in. A number of my best lessons learned about culture and community came from these types of experiences.

Examples of pop up u spaces are barber shops, churches, beauty/nail salons, basketball courts, sneaker boutiques, malls, video games spaces, cafeterias, student union buildings and more.

Places we hosted a Pop Up U
- Barbershop
- Basketball court
- Nail Salon
- The cafeteria
- The mall
- Instagram Live

Steps to Setting up a Pop Up U

1. Identify a location
2. Have a liaison
3. Meet the people where they are
4. Everything is a leadership lesson
5. Embrace being a teacher and a student

CLOUT CHASING LEADERSHIP

CLOUT CHASER. /klout 'CHāsər/ noun. A person who strategically associates themselves with the success of a popular person or a current contemporary trend to gain fame and attention.

Clout chasing has many negative aspects. My students talk about it all the time, while discussing rappers, Instagram stars and even their peers. Clout chasing is nothing new and neither is this theory I'm coining as Clout Leadership. We've been working with clout-having leaders for years, but the strategic component is the key difference.

Clout Leadership is the act of strategically recruiting, then training a student who is popular among their peers on campus and working with them to assist in the development of university wide student leadership.

Student affairs professionals must recognize that they are not the coolest person in the room. There will always be students who resonate to their peers more than you will. They are often nontraditional leaders. They command an audience without an executive board position. Without a title of Resident Assistant or Orientation Leader, people are following their moves.

The appreciation of celebrity culture, although often problematic, will always exist. At your institution, whether they are athletes, gamers or members of Greek Life, celebrities exist. Students with status and no official titles are controlling the pulse of the campus. Cultivating relationships is a skill not often taught and yet we have experts right in our backyard.

Impactful peer to peer interaction is often a learning outcome we seek in our work and it's time to embrace its impact as much as possible.

 Leading psychologist, professor and author of the text, *Popular, The Power of Likeabiltiy in Status Obsessed World*, suggests "in a very real manner, our experiences with popularity are always occupying our minds." A RAND Corporation think tank report also shows how popularity positively impacts academic success. We have to bring that same energy in developing our student leaders.

I am in the business of turning those students into official campus leaders or as close to it as possible. Through education, branding, training and more importantly buy in, we can transform the idea of student leadership. Remember, clout is relative. We have diverse audiences on our campus, so one person's clout is another person's corny. Popularity comes in all shapes, sizes and locations. We have to identify the various pockets and find the big dogs in those areas.

One year, while hiring Orientation Leaders, I strategically recruited all the students with clout I could find. We hired the following students:
- *two sorority sisters who were known for being the best steppers on campus.*
- *the student who ran all the fashion shows and was president of the popular black student union.*
- *the Biology major who presented at all the STEM symposiums.*

These weren't just students who represented particular areas, but they had what we call *the Juice*. Through their work, not only did they help our first year student population get more involved, but they served as the mouth pieces for the leadership and the institution overall.

Case #1

Jack was known around campus for having the nicest car, super exclusive sneakers and an infectious personality. I was introduced to him by another student leader while they were making snap vids.

I hired Jack to be the spokesperson for my office. He promoted the heck out of our events and helped increase the attendance of leadership programs by 2 percent. I can't correlate the jump singlehandedly to his work, but I do know that there were 5 of his friends who never showed face prior and were now regular attendees. Jack himself was recently inducted into our leadership academy.

Case #2

Lauren was easily one the most popular students on campus. It seemed like she knew everybody on campus and then some. She was a star at talent and fashion shows. Students admired her confidence and overall style. She and I built a rapport after many conversations about some of her favorite rappers and street wears. She met all the requirements of being an RA, but nobody ever approached her to apply. I immediately saw the potential as well as the ability to reach the students our office was struggling to connect to. After taking her under my leadership wing, she decided to go for the job and she got it. She was a stellar RA. One of her greatest clout impacts came through Social media. Our twitter account was a fledgling. We then created an account, @LaurenTheRA and the fame changed. She immediately tripled our followers and boosted interactions. Students were going to Lauren's account instead of ours to ask questions about policies, checkouts or programming. She catapulted us into an arena we needed to be.

COUNT YOUR STEPS

A few years back, wearable fitness trackers were super popular and discussed everywhere. The number one question was "How many steps did you take today?" For many, 10,000 steps would be a great day for your personal fitness. Let's flip the narrative to how many meaningful steps are you taking within your position that are culturally responsive.

The steps you take may not get the approval.

Shabazz story:

The first time I ever witnessed a leader wear sneakers was during my time as an admissions counselor. During my daily journeys of recruitment, I saw the principal and vice principal wearing fresh kicks with their suits. Before I could ask, the vice principal let me know the deal. "In our school we are never in our office, so sneakers are essential to our day to day. We take steps and walk throughout the building, making ourselves visible to all. He practiced what he preached. So much so, that our scheduled meeting took place as we walked around the building. We discussed agenda items in the hallways. Strategies were broken down in the cafeteria and ideas were shared by the lockers. During that walk, we met staff and students. A memorable moment took place when a student without a hall pass switched gears right in front of us. I'm not sure if this student was trying to cut class, was late or had another reason to be in the halls. He was immediately upset about the situation he was in, then flipped it on us and became excited over the Vice Principal's fresh kicks. Here was the actual dialogue

Principal: James I need you to get yourself back to class. You know the rules; no walking the halls without a pass.
James: Man, I don't want to be there. Wait, Principal Smith your kicks are fire.
Principal: You know I know the game
James: Respect!

Now right after the student showed love for the kicks, it broke down any tension from leader to student. Both parties felt as though they had common ground and were respectfully on the same level no matter the title. The principal navigated both discipline and relevance to help the student understand not only the rules, but a principal can still be authentic and into the same culture.

Violence and dropout rates plagued this same school before the principal was promoted. At the time, only 46 percent of students were proficient in language arts and just 19 percent in math. Failure had become so commonplace at Shabazz that the state, which now ran Newark schools, was considering shutting the school down when Mills, already a Shabazz vice principal, was elevated to principal in 2011.

At the time, only 46 percent of students were proficient in language arts and just 19 percent in math, according to Mills. But Mills, leaning heavily on the tough-love disciplinary style of the school's charismatic new football coach, Darnell Grant, took the building back.

Over the course of four years, Mills raised the percentage of students proficient in language arts to 74 percent, the highest jump in the city. In math, 37 percent were now proficient. By pushing students to think more seriously about their futures, Mills was able to increase the percentage of graduating seniors matriculating to four-year colleges or universities, from 23 percent to 46 percent.

The use of social learning and cooperative work extends pass k-12. Typically, we have culturally responsive learning within these spaces, but only done in small pockets outside of that space. In our corporation and colleges, the lack of cultural relevance has led to low retention and morale among our teams. Just like Principal Mills, happiness and comfortability can help change those numbers.

After this story, I accounted some steps we can take.

Culturally responsive steps – These are the steps we take to learn other personalities and cultures within our schools, organizations and teams. Those steps are to be a totality of people, practice and policies. For example, visiting departments or spaces were you understand how to treat everyone based on individual experience over cultural assumptions.

It is time to listen to the crowd.

Steps beyond approval- We've tried that before. The budget won't allocate for that next step. Our boss would never go for that. How many times have we heard those voices from our colleagues and inner thoughts? With this step, we must make moves without approval. I remember having a supervisor tell a colleague and I, that they've seen our idea run past the office before it failed. My response, as a former athlete, was sometimes it's not the play but the player within it. The following year, my colleague and I broke the office record for applications and enrollment by using the same idea; different players. As leaders and voices for all backgrounds, we may have to create things the office has never seen before. We are changing as a society; new faces, new cultures and more. Tweaking an old failed system with new players can bring all the success.

Lastly, creativity brings about fear. In life, no one can deny positive results and efficient productivity. Don't wait for financial support, be creative and produce micro results that will get supported and turn into macro success.

THE DEFIANT ONES

HBO's The Defiant Ones documented the history and partnership of Dr. Dre and Jimmy Iovine. The two musical legends took us down memory lane and while doing so, created alternative paths towards leadership. They painted glamorous stories of struggle and triumph. The narrative provided important reminders to the types of diverse personalities and character traits found within any journey to success.

There is no guarantee to becoming a music mogul or multi-millionaire, but defiant people are everywhere. They recognize success when on many occasions, they are unrecognized themselves. Are you ready to dispose of the cultural assumptions that have potentially clouded your viewpoint of others? In education, the workforce and our surrounding communities, we see Defiant Leaders, Defiant staff, Defiant Students and more, elude the trappings of traditional definitions.

I think about the defiant first generation student who reads statistic after statistic, stating their deficiencies. What are you doing as an educator or institution to assist them in their process? Are you making sure these students are taking advantage of your resources? It's one thing to say, "We have a tutoring center or advisement office." The major key is to assure that those students are using them. Don't simply be a bystander, but get in the game of helping students succeed. Jimmy Iovine mentioned that Bruce Springsteen taught him work ethic. At a point within the film after a tough session, co producer Jon Landau states, "Jimmy, you're missing the big picture. What are we here for? We are here to help Bruce make the best record he can. That's the job... We're not here to make you happy, we're not here to make me happy. We're here to contribute to the project and it's Bruce's project."

Leadership is never just about you. The process involves actively engaging diverse audiences. Your statistical assessment alone will not be enough. The push coming from Bruce Springsteen or an excited first generation student, is important to everyone reaching levels once deemed to be unlikely or even impossible.

The **Defiant New Professional,** was a star within the college ranks only 3 months ago.

Today, they are nervous about that first job. The profession doesn't always match the degree. They are the low person on that totem and the lack of confidence is impacting their ability to leave a mark. The pressure builds and, at times, they overcompensate for fear of what the future may bring. As leaders whether serving as mentors or supervisors, we have to cultivate new professionals who are willing to learn and willing to work. There's some unwritten myth that once you've received one or two degrees, the learning stops. Watching Dr. Dre's progression within the documentary is an excellent example of growth and development. He started as a DJ, transitioned into a producer and rapper, then finally into a record executive and business mogul. Iovine, in talking about his work, said "My proudest thing in my career is that I was able to change it three times. And I'm happy about that, I couldn't have done the same thing my whole life, I would've gone nuts."

The Defiant New Professional isn't always ready for the position they are currently holding, but that doesn't mean the situation is a total loss. Provide this new person with opportunities that have measurable results. Tangible outcomes are more effective than lofty goals and ambiguous mission statements. Hurdles happen every day and as leaders, we've got to remind others that a slow start, trip, fall or obstacles doesn't end the world.

One of my favorite Defiant Non Traditional students was a 45 year old immigrant mother. English was her fourth language. I hired her as a math tutor and took some heat for that. People were concerned about relatability, others felt that there were going to be language barriers. She also didn't always get along with her fellow staff members. She had a stellar academic record and during our interview, she said to me that "I will be great no matter what appears in front of me." She came to this country and people doubted her. She wore a hijab and people gave her side eyes. She defied all odds against her, picked up a bachelor's as an adult learner then a master's degree and currently serves as a college professor. *The Defiant Non Traditional* student is among the strongest you'll ever meet. In the documentary, Jimmy Iovine took a chance on acts like Gerardo, Primus and Dr. Dre, all of which helped his label become successful. Whenever you judge a book by its cover, you'll end up realizing that you can't read at all.

The Defiant Inventor

A former staff member of mine openly hated 80 percent of their job. They couldn't deal with the daily administrative duties, were frustrated with the bureaucracy from the top, had issues with other coworkers, and more. This person enjoyed two things; building with the students and even more so, coming up with cool ideas to innovate the office and programs. They were all ideas all the time.

Help them stay creative even when the ideas aren't always being accepted. When plans and implementations are moving slow, push forward.

There is a **Defiant Student Leader** out there who needs our support. They aren't sure how to articulate their goals to the masses. They want to challenge the institution but are fearful of potential repercussions. We have to be there for them. Students have come into my office ready to be change agents that leave a legacy on campus, but are clueless to the steps. These are the ones who are labeled lazy but with potential. Other students have followed them to the party, but have not walked with them to the president's office or marched alongside them within the parade. They have the personality and the want, now it's our job to provide the guidance and know how, that will turn them into leaders of their peers. I love student leaders because so many have the gift but are a bit rough around the edges. To see their growth and eventual transformation into people who are going to potentially change the world, or at minimum their campus, is a beautiful sight. Never give up on them.

The Defiant student community are all around us. They are transgender, black women, military veterans, disabled, LatinX, Resident Assistants and athletes. They are professionals sending money back home to their family in native countries. They are people who have switched their career trajectories at an age older than they expected. They are those who pulled up that first semester 1.9 GPA to a 3.5 by graduation. The have 3 jobs to support their family, all while taking 21 credits as a Biochem major. They are the women, men and people who make our jobs as educators that much more special than so many other professions.

THE LOGIN PROCESS

We're really comfortable with what it means to be a follower. On Instagram, Tik Tok, Snapchat, Twitter and other social media platforms, everyone supports the value of a follow, but not so many people are about the role of a leader. On the other hand, away from social media, the concept of leadership is taught all across the board. We see it in classrooms, offices, conferences, books, graduate programs and more. Often left out of that conversation is following within actual life. A social media society leaves you numb as a follower. The screens invite you to get lost in colors, images and words without full recognition of where you truly are. We scroll and click away, aimlessly at times, with hopes of finding something we never were looking for to begin with.

When talking about the obsession of mindless or non-essential following, it is just as important for us to teach people what it means to be a good follower. There can't be great leaders if we're in a room with poor followers. Everyone needs to understand how their roles play a part. Getting the best out of what should be a reciprocal relationship, involves a few qualities.

My mother asked me to set up an Uber account for her. She had never used the app before and was initially clueless, despite being able to log in. If I left her to her devices to try understand how it all works, she would struggle mightily. Do your followers, students, staff or constituents know what they are getting into? Have you explained how to properly navigate the space? Anyone can get into the platform but true success won't happen unless clarity has been created on how to move accordingly. One can't expect followers to move effectively through a space that's unknown to them. It is not fair to place blame on followers while the leaders themselves haven't worked to assure the competency levels are where they need to be to succeed. Create clear guidelines in defining your goals and any tasks that need to be defined. Don't be afraid to have conversations and ask the right questions with all involved. Find out how much people know and let that assist you in your leadership. Caring about how competent others are is a sign that you are committed to being culturally responsive.

Filters

Filters are used to change colors, lighting and photo effects. They are made to add some flavor to a pic. They are truly augmenting reality. Honesty differentiates the real from the filter. Honesty reflections with the leader about what is being portrayed, are necessary for transparent development. If I am always posting filters so much so that my audience cannot tell the difference between what's real and what's altered, the message will never hit its goal. When creating new lighting, adding masks and shades and altering backgrounds become a priority, how can I expect people to not get fooled? Trust gets lost when the followers are uncertain about the consistency in the space. Ultimately, filters do not last forever and there will be a moment when the true side comes out. It is at that point where those receiving the message will rebel.

As a follower, I have to be able to look and watch carefully so that I am not constantly being duped into believing that filters are reality. It is important for me to know what natural light looks like. It is important for me to know what your face looks like. It's important for me to know what your background looks like, so that whenever a filter comes on I can differentiate between the two. We all have to be in tune with the idea of authentic stories.

Follow back

Whenever we ask students to follow us on social media, they almost always ask us if they're going to get a follow back. Leadership is a reciprocal process. We have a responsibility to create meaningful exchanges that elevate as many people in our space as possible. Hierarchy and positions give people a sense of power, but in reality you can't lead unless you are giving back. Followers as well, can't simply take and take without an expectation of putting in some work. While creating culturally responsive environments, it is important that all parties involved are benefiting from the leadership being delivered. Following back means we are willing to push each other to be great.

I would tell students that I only follow back people who are posting positivity and creating dope energy. We both have to walk away with something to gain and something to give. No matter your position, leadership should never be a one way street. Pay attention to your interactions. Are they respectful? Are you valuing the voices of others during important exchanges?

Following back is ultimately a sign of respect for everyone involved.

Selfies

Kanye West once rapped, "It's hard to stay humble when you're stuntin on a Jumbotron". In a world full of selfies, it's just as difficult to practice selflessness on a phone screen. It's easy to always look at yourself and take pics until it's perfect. To engage in the art of following requires a dedication to humility. It is essential to acknowledge what you don't know and not be afraid to ask those in the room for help. As a leader, one must also sacrifice their own egos to be able to exist with others. In educational spaces you not only have to recognize everyone in the space that you are sharing, but also acknowledge their excellence and everything else they bring to the table. That first selfie isn't always perfect. Sometimes the photo we seek is best taken by others. Taking less selfies, in this case, means a commitment to collective movement. The journey involves levels of trust that can't be completed with one singular view. Your students add not only different viewpoints, but they remind the viewers of the work that's being done.

When making key decisions about policy, remember it's not about you. Learning processes cannot be cultivated alone.

Repost

Including everyone in the process of leadership will allow the work to go beyond you. Giving followers a role in which they are engaged and involved in the overall growth and development, encourages them to "repost." When one properly reposts on Instagram they not only spread the word to their audience but, also provide credit to the original poster.

Not everyone is capable of spreading the message. This isn't always the fault of the follower. I'm always asking myself if I provided the students or staff with the tools not only needed to succeed, but continue with the transfer of energy, power or messaging. Be aware of what resources are available. Clarity in how you deliver and follow up to confirm all interpretations are clear, makes all the difference in how far your reach is.

Instagram accounts we follow:

@earnyourleisure - *The power of creating a platform that provides collective information and success.* As educators and people, sometimes our ego stops us from inviting expert voices from all fields into the room. This platform not only adds people, but adds valuable education lessons from industry leaders. This shows the best teacher does not always have a strong research based academic background. It literally takes doing the work.

@maudiepooh - *The ability to spread leadership through a passion.* Maud and her sister, equally as powerful leaders on social media, provide empowerment through tap. The digital leadership lesson is to show that many of our passions have valuable learning lessons and leadership skills within them. Even more is trusting that your superpower can be valuable to a niche market.

@jacobmotivisch – *The generational mentor excels.* He is an amazing photographer. We met him as a student and since then has shot multiple photos featured in the New York Times.

@Iamashcash - *the power of ownership.* Ash Cash is someone we personally met years ago wearing Timberlands and a suit. Authenticity to the fullest. What was even more unique than his amazing energy was his profession. At the time Ash Cash was a CEO of a Credit Union in Harlem, NY. Credit Unions were rare in the neighborhood, not to mention one that was owned by a black man. Ash Cash has created lanes and owned his voice. As of today, he is now running his own morning show via IGTV. He is a decorated and bestselling author who brings it every time. Despite being denied by gatekeepers for "too much energy", he is defying the odds with his ability to innovate through ownership.

THE MARSHAWN LYNCH
FACTOR

"I'm just here so I don't get fined"
-    *Marshawn Lynch*

The NFL fines anyone who doesn't sit with reporters during pre and post-game interviews. Marshawn Lynch was not here for the pageantry and proceeded to get fined. In response to the punishment, Lynch decided to sit for the questions but provided this one simple answer to whatever was asked, "I'm just here so I don't get fined". This isn't an indictment on Lynch as a leader or a football player. He was beloved by his teammates and extremely productive on the field. This was a representation of protest to something he was mandated to do. It was his way of saving some extra money and to avoid fines. By spitting those words, he technically met the requirements but the substance being sought out by the league didn't happen.

In leadership we have some talented individuals who understand how to grow, lead and make a difference. Unfortunately, some of those same people are at jobs, institutions, in offices or on teams in which they are simply there so they don't get fined. Their reason isn't an open protest, but rather an apathy towards their work. Getting fined in these cases could mean the following:

- I'm just here so I don't get fired.
- I'm just here because they pay me to be.
- I'm just here because there's nothing better to do.
- I'm just here because I can't find another job.

In the field of education, such a mindset is not only problematic professionally, but more importantly, a detriment to the students being served. Beyond the realm of education, these thoughts are toxic to your team and students, and your developmental growth as a leader or employee.

A former coworker of mine, Ursula, came to work every day no matter what. The good days, sick days, the long days, she was there. We would ride the bus in the morning or take the walk to office on nice days. She worked in a scholarship office working with alumni and identifying scholarship opportunities for students. She enjoyed work but was never seeing opportunity for growth. Ursula was passed over for promotions on multiple occasions and rarely was granted funding or opportunity for professional development. She was promised chances for change but nothing came to fruition. The frustration set in and suddenly she was missing the bus in the morning. I would get a text that she wasn't coming in because she wasn't "feeling it." I'd send students to her office or connect them via email and Ursula was answering more slowly and was less present. When I asked if she'd checked out, she jokingly responded, "I'm here so I don't get fined". The party was over.

My suggestion for these situations is to start the process of finding a new job. It is not good for your spirit to continue doing something you hate, especially when it's impacting something you love. Additionally, remember why you are doing the job. Marshawn did the mandated interviews but more importantly he represented for the people who mattered most. In your work, remember who your most important constituents are. As educators, the students are the priority.

- Avoid joining committees so that you don't have to do extra work.
- Never arrive a minute before you are required and never stay a minute after. In fact you show up late and leave early.
- Intentionally not adding any input to meetings, planning or discussion.
- You put the least amount of effort necessary just to get by.

"I'm bout that action boss"

My favorite Marshawn Lynch quote is, "I'm bout that action boss". Saying this as a leader, is a display of readiness for all changes, oncoming detractors and more. It signifies that someone is prepared to do the tough work as well as the simple tasks.

The Stiff Arm - In football the goal of the stiff arm is to thwart away any would-be tacklers. It is a move that's not about being elusive but rather, a display that you are prepared to deliver some hits yourself. You are searching for some contact. There are moments where we have to be a bit more forward as leaders. Sitting back can get you and so many others left behind. A culturally responsive stiff arm is an assurance that people are discussing the necessary needs of students or others whose voices are not being considered as part of the process. It's not always going to result in the touchdown you seek because decision makers make calls. I've sat on search committees, curriculum development committees, student success groups, and more in which I didn't have the last say and my choices or philosophy didn't always match the final decision. Despite that, my stiff arm was always felt. My voice was always heard.

The professional stiff arm;

- You speak up in rooms where marginalized voices are being left out and stiff arm archaic and traditional mindsets.
- You take on roles with the intention of being a change agent.
- You actively go search for other people who are also looking to create change.
- You actively participate in professional development opportunities and do the work on your own even if the space doesn't want you to.

- You ask challenging questions that force people to deeply investigate potential choices and decisions.

The first down

Incremental change counts and so do large scale shifts. Be prepared to do both. Sometimes a single yard can change momentum of entire game. In the same vein, simple changes can impact an entire work environment. Within my office, I created a no eating in the office policy. It was a small act, but such a move forced staff members to leave their desks. It allowed them to not get bogged down at the desk and to create a self-mandate to walk away. One of the bigger aspects of the change was forcing the staff members to interact with the community more. My staff now have more conversations with students in the cafeteria or student union building. They are collaborating more due to lunch meetings happening, scheduled or otherwise. This one yard first down play in my office has a great opportunity to create larger impact on the staff and institution as a whole.

DON'T GET LEFT

I've lived in New York City for most of my life. Visiting the borough of Manhattan was always fun until it was time to go home. Between the years 2006-2012, I lived in both Brooklyn and the Bronx. Getting a yellow cab to take me home was always an adventure. By adventure I mean a terrible experience. Cab drivers would refuse to travel to Brooklyn or claim the Bronx was too far a drive. Not to mention as a black man, the struggle was real no matter the destination. Yellow cabs were synonymous with New York City. They ran above ground transportation and acted as biased or racist as they wanted to. Then it happened. One of the emblematic signs of NYC started to get left. Ride hailing apps like Uber, Lyft, Via, Juno and Gett came through the door and immediately made their presence known.

That wave of the future will never stop approaching. The choice is to adapt and ride it out (no pun intended) or drown. NYC yellow cabs thought things were all good and suddenly found themselves under water. According to the New York Times, the medallions that give cabs the right to operate have plummeted in value, going for less than half of the $1.3 million price recorded in 2013 and 2014. By the time they figured out what was happening and started creating their own taxi apps, the momentum had left them in the dust. In fact, I have friends who are recent NYC transplants and have never seen the inside of a yellow cab.

There may be some laws being implemented to save yellow cabs, but it might be too late. Nobody is above getting left. Blockbuster Video, Toys R Us, Macy's, Major League Baseball, and so many other companies and individuals failed to recognize the situations they found themselves placed in.

For your own growth and development, it's important to continually be culturally responsive. Recognize the trends and think about personal relationships to the present and the future. If part of your decision making process regularly includes phrases like, "when I was younger we never did that" or "back in my day, things were better," and "it's never worked like that before," you're a Sucka MC.

Criticizing younger generations for no other reason than them being different than the past, also makes you a Sucka MC. To find true success, one must be prepared to learn things they aren't familiar with. To excel is to evolve. Being around college students on a regular basis has been an ever evolving learning process. They've taught me about the newest trends all while putting me on to unfamiliar perspectives. The learning process is reciprocal. As mentioned earlier within the text, they are my generational mentors. The learning process is fully reciprocal.

Innovation will continue to change business markets. For your own personal success, not only be prepared for disruption, but always be ready to adapt and grow. Sucka MCs will be stuck on that porch trying to figure out what year it is.

The Disorientation of Getting Left

1. *Disorient yourself from the arrogance that outshines your innovation*

Nothing stops innovation and growth like arrogance. Arrogance will hold you back from working with new ideas and people. Mike Tyson is attributed to the quote, "Everybody has a plan until they get punched in the face". The arrogant minded don't even think they could get punched at all. Don't get knocked out and then fail to get up and innovate because of a belief that your shit don't stink. It always does, my friend, always.

2. *Disorient yourself from the "traditional" mindsets*

Traditional mindsets were often created when only one voice was allowed to be in the room. There was most likely a lack of diversity in looks and thoughts. Such traditions have survived the times with no rhyme or reason, existing simply because time and history says so. Those who benefit from traditional views that exclude others are Sucka MCs and will try anything to hold on to their one time advantage. We must disorient ourselves from the archaic.

Heteronormative, racist, misogynistic views are the perfect recipes for getting left.

In the following pages, we'll present case studies in which we have disrupted traditional leadership spaces.

Don't Get Left Case Study #1
Lemonade Meets the Social Change Model

The Social Change Model of Leadership was developed in 1994. Till this day, colleges and universities refer to this model as their primary method of student leadership and development. As we worked with student leaders at many institutions, it was visibly noticeable how much boredom was being exhibited by them while being trained using the Social Change Model. There are integral moments within it where pertinent information is displayed, but 20 plus years after its inception, once could argue the shine was getting dim.

Beyoncé dropped her chart-topping album and video project, Lemonade on April 23, 2016. About two weeks later, we dropped our article entitled Lemonade Meets the Social Change Model. We took an older idea and flipped it. Traditional standards can be changed with some culturally responsive methodology. From our students to our fellow colleagues, everyone was listening to and paying to Beyoncé at that moment.

To make this happen, it is essential to be knowledgeable on two fronts. The restructuring of archaic ideas requires an understanding of the work and research, and additionally, a dedication to include the voice of the relevant into that space. One doesn't need to force the matter, but find points of congruence.

Don't Get Left Case Study 2
The NCSL Change

The National Conference on Student Leadership has been around since 1978. For decades, it's been regarded as one of the top student leadership conferences in the country. They've always had great workshops and talented speakers. As the years moved forward, there were some transitions in conference directors, and the content started to get stagnant in certain areas. They needed a jolt and as timing would have it, we were available.

Including Career Readiness into Leadership

We recognized that a key component of leadership development was providing students with the tools needed to succeed on and off campus. Research continues to suggest the importance of college students having tangible skills and being prepared for the workforce. We added professional development blocks into the conference featuring workshops covering areas such as negotiation tactics, interview skills and more. Other breakout moments included résumé review, cleaning up of LinkedIn pages along with professional headshots for each student.

Leadership Day Party

The Leadership Day Party is an event we created to switch up the way opening ceremonies and welcome sessions are facilitated. Who says leadership can't be fun? Our first step was including a DJ. The sound system with a cool playlist was functional. Having a DJ, with the ability to read the crowd, switch and blend songs when needed, on booming speakers was transformative. Instead of the usual icebreakers and traditional opening comments, we added a bit more flavor. Students were networking with the Migos and Bruno Mars in the background. Students were doing the latest

dances while discussing inclusion and
diversity.

Shorter Keynote Speeches

Keynote speeches were always an hour at this
conference. Great speakers can fill up an
hour easily, but even the best must compete
with the distractions of cell phones, social
media and overall decline in attention spans.
We noticed that and rearranged the format of
the hour. We added a Q&A within the
speeches and encouraged speakers to add
some activity into their time. Additionally,
we shied away from traditional motivational
speakers and included professionals, and
storytellers who provided a different type of
narrative for the students.

Don't Get Left Case Study 3
Workshops and Articles

When Trill or Not Trill started as a blog, we
were committed to writing pieces that
resonated from both pop culture and
educational space. We did the same with our
workshops. It meant that we had to stay fresh
and knowledgeable, not only about what was
happening in the world, but also in higher
education. Here are a few of the most
popular presentations and articles we created
at the start of Trill or Not Trill.

Title: *Leadership Typologies According to Scandal*

Description: This workshop used the popular television show, Scandal, as a vehicle to teach lessons on different leadership typologies. We broke down character traits and referenced particular scenes, all while using research based leadership strategies.

Presented to: National Association of Campus Activities, New Jersey City University, Long Island University, St. John's University.

Title: *Turning Criticism into Greatness: The Study of Steph Curry*

Description: Steph Curry's career started out with many doubters, as he had to overcome injuries and slumps. He flipped that into a Hall of Fame career with multiple MVPs and championships. We used specific news articles, statistics and video content as materials used to discuss early academic struggles, student success and overall involvement as a leader on campus.

Presented to: University of Maryland, Kean University

THE STUDENTS

Without the students, we would not be where we are today. They are the largest inspiration to the work that gets done at the Trill or Not Trill Institute. We would be remiss not to mention some of those who have pushed us to new heights, as well as those who have directly been impacted by the specific culturally responsive curriculum and training program we've provided. The following students have studied and trained with us.

Alvert Hernandez was a 1st generation high school, college and grad school graduate of Dominican and Cuban descent. The child of a single, teenage mother, he began his college career with uncertainty struggling early on. While working directly with members of the Trill or Not Trill Team, Alvert's leadership skills were honed over 2 years of direct skill building. He improved his public speaking, as well as interview and writing skills. Alvert's confidence was boosted by being encouraged to present at conferences and eventually plan his own as Student Government President. He later graduated from New Jersey City University and went on to become a star graduate student at Montclair State University. He continued to work with Trill or Not Trill and recently accepted a position as Assistant Director of Residence Life at Ursinus College. Currently, Alvert also presents at conferences and institutions nationwide on topics including LatinX leadership, Teamwork and more.

"Trill or Not Trill helped me become a better student by challenging me to take on new and larger roles on campus. They helped prepare me for my professional career not only through their innovative workshops, but by providing me with opportunities to speak at national conferences and increased my overall skills as a well-balanced educator. They are a major reason why I am successfully working as a Student Affairs professional today at Ursinus College"

-Alvert Hernandez

Arijean Feliciano

As a single teenage mother, Arijean Feliciano put her college dreams on hold. But after she was laid off from work, Arijean decided to go back to college, ending a 14 year hiatus. It was there she met the co-founders of Trill or Not Trill. She worked with them to improve her skills within the fields of entrepreneurship and leadership. Trill or Not Trill helped Arijean become a better presenter and an overall student. She was encouraged to engage in new endeavors as a nontraditional student and proceeded to excel. She graduated as a respected leader and immediately moved into a professional career. Arijean currently serves as a Security Master Representative at Fidelity Investment and continues to use the skills she learned from Trill or Not Trill while diligently working on various committees. She's even implemented some of her learnings in her own household. Her son recently graduated from high school and is on way to becoming a great student leader himself.

"My experience as a student leader and working with Trill or Not Trill, was rewarding and led me to have the confidence to be myself in the workplace and excel in the corporate environment. I would be remiss if I did not say that Trill or Not Trill had a bigger impact than others."

- *Arijean Feliciano*

Bailey Synclaire

Bailey was a student at the university of Missouri. While there, she was a member of the school's TRiO Program. TRiO is a federal outreach program designed to provide services for individuals from disadvantaged backgrounds. It was there she met her mentor who opened the door of opportunities. One of those opportunities was traveling to Washington D.C. for the National Conference on Student Leadership. While working with Trill or Not Trill, not only did Bailey challenge the team, but she also received the push to be her best. She was a midwestern native with dreams of moving to New York City or Los Angeles to pursue her dreams in media. While working with Trill or

Not Trill, she cleaned up her résumé, took numerous leadership courses and even facilitated a partnership with us and the University of Missouri. She took part in regular coaching calls where she continued to gain the motivation to reach her goals. Bailey eventually made her way to New York City and landed a job at Comedy Central. She has produced her own short films, worked on viral influencer content, moderated panels, and more.

FROM PIVOT TO EURO STEP LEADERSHIP

As we close this text, we would be remiss to not mention the pandemic that changed the world of education, leadership and beyond. Covid-19 forced every industry to quickly adapt. Education was not spared from the ever-evolving unpredictability of the virus. The crisis was multidimensional and continued to require culturally responsive and adaptive leadership. Everyone began pivoting in attempt to prepare. That was the popular term and strategy seen from various sectors. The idea is to take a turn into a direction different from your original while remaining planted. These changes were not overly drastic but were more so incremental, while normalcy served as a backdrop and foundation.

A friend of ours did their best HaHa Davis impersonation while discussing their institution, "our campus finna change but not change, change." In essence, adjustments were coming but theory, thought and practice would remain the same in many ways. A new computer program or Zoom account won't mean much if your mindset and policies don't change.

In basketball, a pivot is defined as *the action of stepping with one foot while keeping the other foot at its point of contact with the floor.* There is no true transformational movement happening. In our work, the pivot wasn't enough. We chose to hit the world with some Euro Step Leadership.

In basketball, this is *a two-step move intended to allow the offensive player to evade a defender and attack the basket.* The Euro Step's goal is to be proactive in the attempt to score. It involves flexibility, focus, changes in pace if done well, and finishing with a score. At Trill Or Not Trill, Euro Step Leadership is a strategic move of being simultaneously adaptive and progressive in thought, theory and action. We wanted to evade as many hurdles as possible and focus on how to reshape traditional plans of actions.

The EuroStep Leadership plan includes these 4 F's:

Understand the **FORECAST**
Embrace **FELLOWSHIP**
Alternative **FUNDING**
FOCUS on the big picture

Understand the Forecast

The five-day forecast isn't always perfect, but it is predictive. When that meteorologist or weather person tells you that the rest of the week is going to be sunny, it's a beautiful sight to see. At the same time, the forecast also predicts the rain or cold. You're reminded that this upcoming Wednesday just might require an umbrella. The following day is winter coat season. With sunshine comes rain as well. The willingness and ability to recognize the good, the bad and ugly in your field is a major factor towards being constantly ready to reach success and adapt when necessary.

Understanding the forecast isn't a magic trick or random bet. The assessment and research are everything. Since our inception, Trill Or Not Trill watched the fluctuating trends within higher education. Students were looking at alternative learning options and certification programs. People were questioning their return on investments as tuition prices went up. Generation Z were digital natives who were comfortable with technology, wanted an improved online experience. The U.S. birthdate has continuously dropped causing an impending dip in college enrollment. All these sentiments and actions were demonstrations of a shift approaching. We didn't see a global pandemic coming but what we did see, was a change in the educational horizon.

Our process of moving forward addressed those concerns mentioned earlier.

Launched A New Online Program

We launched a brand new online leadership platform for students to gain particular skills they might be missing out on due to changes in programming and curriculum on their campuses. The program focuses on leadership, communication, career readiness and social justice. The goal is to create an additional opportunity for students to succeed outside of the classroom. It is interactive and will involve multiple platforms already familiar to students. In addition, we will be launching a similar platform which will enable educators who may be struggling to cope with the changes, create ideas for their students or who may be seeking to network more effectively with their peers.

Technology Ready

When the world went virtual, we were ready. Although it wasn't something we often used, we both had lighting, microphones and web cams ready to go before speaking to any new online audience. Understanding the forecast, we were planning to create more online content when suddenly the world of education moved to Zoom or Microsoft Teams. A month into most campuses shutting down, finding a proper microphone or webcam became increasingly difficult. Having access to the technology, helped elevate the way we presented to audiences and opened the door to more opportunities.

Alternative Funding

Budget cuts are the most dreadful news to deliver to an innovative leader. With that in mind, sometimes a budget cut can spark some ideas. This point brings me to March 2020, a year with a fantastic upside and opportunity for TONT until COVID came. We lost out on numerous speaking gigs due to cancellations. The largest conference in higher education had selected us to be presenters and speakers that month and in the blink of any eye, it was gone. We had a limited budget and no real opportunities in the interim.

Immediately, we sat down and had a brainstorming session for ages. Hours of thinking about the next step led us to a few conclusions. This goes back to the understanding the forecast. We recognized that low budgets meant people were looking for resources, empathy, and skills for free. So, we did just that. An underrated concept is being human based rather than transactional. Many of our peers temporarily shut down because of cancelled contracts and choosing to pivot instead of euro stepping. Colleagues were talking about Covid-19 as a crisis that would cripple educational leadership and student development from practitioners. We knew that maintaining a relationship was the most important. Outside of education, this is known as social currency. The result of cashing in on our social currency was a plan that changed our business forever. Our ability to maintain and strengthen relationships was all the funding we needed.

We can't talk about social currency without provided tips around what we discovered.

1. **Understand the pulse of your field**
   The pulse of any place without a budget is exhausted. Whether that's sweat equity or mental drainage, individuals lack innovation when they are tired. It is time to provide resources and fill in the gap. Many folks needed digital programs in colleges, so TONT shared a free branded resource guide. Providing this resource helped colleges and students significantly along the way.

2. **Stand by your word**.
   If you're empathic in words, be empathic in action. Don't be

someone who only shows care on a social media post but won't support those in need in person.

3. **Slide in the DM.**
   Justin Brown, a Student Affairs Professional, booked 56 guests with a $0 budget. There was no secret recipe besides outreach. So many influencers want to teach others for free. They understand their influence and the power of relationship building. Personalize each dm. I've sent over 547 DMs(Direct messages) since June but only netted 49 responses. That is a response rate of 9%, which to our team is better than 0%. Be flexible in your outreach and use all platforms. As the students would say, "shoot your shot." A Pop culture figure loved by students is more accessible to book virtually than in-person; and in most cases, more affordable as well.

The funding will always be there if your social currency is large and expansive.

Continue creating valuable relationships that benefit beyond the dollar amount.

Embrace fellowship

Many will try to pivot on their own. Trill Or Not Trill has never subscribed to this solo mission mentality. Our organization was built on two brothers putting egos aside and joining forces. This decision immediately improved our individual capabilities as well as enhanced the development of the group. As the world changed, we knew surviving alone wasn't an option. The conduit was being built before a pandemic showed. Through its inception, Trill Or Not Trill has developed informal and professional relationships with a multitude of talented individuals from various fields of expertise. When facing unpredictability, unreliable information, and changes in rules, all the while expecting to remain successful, your days become daunting. Collective decision-making and strategic partnerships with fellow change agents create more energy to innovate.

As the world of education went remote and the world was reminded yet again of racial injustice's continuous negative impact, we turned to our colleagues. Trill Or Not Trill's Anti-Racist Training Lab was born, less than a month after George Floyd was murdered. We were already working on bias, race, and diversity but knew we needed more. The pivot is to continue sharing our efforts and teaching the community of staffs and students. The explosive euro step leadership move was to assemble a group and create a more comprehensive training opportunity. We reached out via text, email and instagram to folks already doing the work and we did the work together. The list included the following:

- UCLA Law Professor
- Renowned social activist, public theologian, writer and international speaker.
- Licensed Clinician and Psychology Professor
- Veteran Higher Education professional and successful Instagram influencer

- Former High School Principal and cultural competency and STEM consultant
- Nationally Recognized Public speaker
- A spoken word champion and poet laureate

Find the people who you can professionally fellowship with. Identify similarities in the works of others and outline what a mutually beneficial partnership looks like. Winning on your own is a recipe for failure. We've partnered with an old friend turned successful DJ, and an independent studio to create a hugely successful leadership program. We've worked with brilliant Ed Tech Entrepreneurs and educators to enhance our standard programs. The list of collaborators continues to grow and so does the reach and development of Trill or Not Trill.

Focus on the Big Picture

Your professional big picture includes the students, employees, teammates, and those individuals that make your institutions tick. You can't find transformative success without their input or their success in mind. At Trill Or Not Trill, we have always focused on the students. As much as we enjoyed using educators, practitioners, influencers and celebs to deliver leadership lessons, we know amplifying the student's voices is key. The students are the foreseeable future and will continually provide the overarching story of why we do this work. On campuses, we witnessed universities pointing the finger directly at students, when in reality it was their near-sighted views and slow pivots that literally drove people to protest or leave the institution all together.

In creating a series of online programming, the first group of people we wanted to speak to were students. Our first guest, Jael Kerandi from the University of Minnesota was brilliant from start to finish. Jael made headlines for convincing the school to alter its relationship with the Minneapolis Police Department directly following the killing of George Floyd. Jael was excited to be interviewed via zoom which brought in over 75 college/university leaders into the room. Her courage and voice reminded us all of the power of our students. The power of learning and creating action within the now. Better still, she showed us the importance of getting the work done and keeping the big picture in mind despite the dark cloud around that time. It reminded others of the importance of listening and empowering students to speak up about what's wrong in any situation.

When we use the term "culturally responsiveness" we are not referring to pop culture. It is not a hip hop thing despite our company name, it is instead an approach to leadership that empowers the students intellectually, socially, emotionally, and politically. By using current cultural references to engage and teach, we seek to impact the lives of generations to come.

The marathon continues and the work will never stop.

About the Authors

Jeff Dess is an author of six books and is a seasoned professional in higher education. Lenny is a professor within the business departments at multiple institutions, with an MBA.

Both men have traveled nationwide and abroad as public speakers, educators, and co-founders of the Leadership Institute, Trill or Not Trill which focuses on culturally responsive leadership and student development.

They have spoken to over 500,000 students at colleges, universities, conferences, barbershops, pizzerias and more. Between the two of them, they have appeared on CBS, Fox 5 New York, TedX, The Boston Globe, Ebony Magazine, Black Enterprise, The Root, and Hot 97. From working with, consulting and presenting for the NFL, TEDX, Twitter, Buzzfeed, NASPA, NCSL, and The NSLS, these two have continually pushed the envelope when it comes to impacting all those they meet.

Now we must say, Lenny is a Chicago Bulls Fan and Jeff continues to painfully root for the New York Knicks but for some reason they are still great friends and colleagues who are dedicated to changing the world of higher education and beyond.

Books by Jeff Dess

Trill Motivation
Deconstructing Ratchet
We Can See Your Privates
Haiku from the Home of Reverend Mofo Jones
do not hold doors

For More Information, Visit

www.TrillOrNotTrill.com

Made in the USA
Middletown, DE
04 October 2020

21080856R20073